INDY CARS

MARYSA STORM

BLACK
RABBIT
BOOKS

Bolt Jr. is published by Black Rabbit Books
P.O. Box 3263, Mankato, Minnesota, 56002.
www.blackrabbitbooks.com
Copyright © 2020 Black Rabbit Books

Michael Sellner, designer; Omay Ayres, photo researcher

Names: Storm, Marysa, author.
Title: Indy cars / by Marysa Storm.
Description: Mankato, Minnesota : Black Rabbit Books,
[2020] | Series: Bolt Jr. Wild rides | Includes bibliographical
references and index. | Audience: Age 6-8. | Audience:
Grade K to 3.
Identifiers: LCCN 2019002812 (print) | LCCN 2019004647
(ebook) | ISBN 9781623101947 (e-book) |
ISBN 9781623101886 (library binding) |
ISBN 9781644661208 (paperback)
Subjects: LCSH: Indy cars–Juvenile literature.
Classification: LCC TL236.25 (ebook) | LCC TL236.25 .S76
2020 (print) | DDC 629.228/5–dc23
LC record available at https://lccn.loc.gov/2019002812

Printed in the United States. 5/19

Image Credits

Alamy: Igor Vidyashev, 4; behance.net: Ryan Long, 14–15; Corbis:
© Celso Bayo/Fotoarena/Corbis, 13; David Hahn/Icon Sportswire,
1; DieCastModels.co: Chris Biertzer, 10; indymotorspeedway.com:
Indy Speedway, 8–9; markplourderacing.com: Mark Plouder, Cover
(car); Shutterstock: Action Sports Photography, 12, 18–19, 20–21;
Darren Brode, 10–11; Doug James, 7; grafixx, 3, 24; jamesteohart,
Cover; Jon Nicholls Photography, 5, 6–7, 22–23; HodagMedia,
16–17, 21

Contents

Chapter 1

A Powerful Car 4

Chapter 2

In Action 10

Chapter 3

Winning Big 16

More Information 22

A Powerful Car

Indy cars race around a track. They slow for a turn. Then they speed up. Their **engines** scream. Each driver hopes his or her car is the fastest.

engine: a machine that changes energy into mechanical motion

COMPARING
TOP SPEEDS

Indy car ◄ · · · · · · · · ·

about 235 miles
(378 km)
per hour

Reaching Top Speeds

Indy cars are strong race cars.

They're light. And they're very, very fast.

They reach 235 miles (378 kilometers)

per hour.

▶ **stock car**
about 200 miles
(322 km)
per hour

PARTS OF AN

Indy Car

cockpit

front wing

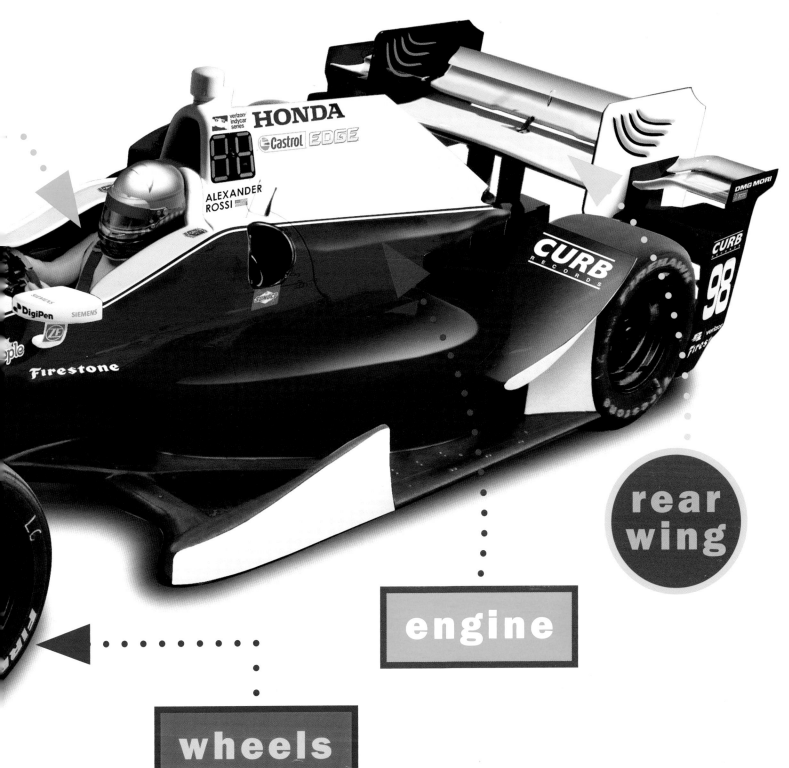

rear wing

engine

wheels

CHAPTER 2

In Action

Not all Indy car races are the same.

Some happen on tracks. In others, cars

speed along tight city streets.

Races begin with a green flag. The first

car to **complete** all **laps** wins.

complete: to finish

lap: one time around or over a course

FACT

The Indy 500 is a popular race. Cars race around an oval track.

11

Safety

Racing is **dangerous**. Crashes can be deadly. For safety, drivers wear helmets and suits. Cars are built for safety too. In crashes, they break apart. This design keeps drivers safe.

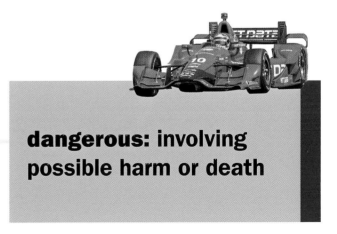

dangerous: involving possible harm or death

Popular Indy Car Races

North America

Road America Grand Prix (Wisconsin)

Toronto Honda Indy (Toronto)

ABC Supply 500 (Pennsylvania)

Indy 500 (Indiana)

CHAPTER 3

Winning Big

After races, drivers get points. Drivers who finish first get the most. Drivers want the most points when the season ends. The driver with the most is champion.

FACT

Indy cars look like Formula 1 cars. Indy cars are faster.

Super Strong

Racing began in the early 1900s. Since then, cars have changed. They've gotten safer. They've also gotten faster. Fans can't wait to see what happens next.

Indy Car's Height
about 40 inches
(102 centimeters)

Bonus Facts

Thirty-three **cars race** at the Indy 500.

During races, tires get very hot. They melt a little.

Early Indy cars had engines in the front.

The cars' **engines are** turbocharged.

turbocharged: having a device that increases an engine's power

21

READ MORE/WEBSITES

Adamson, Thomas K. *Indy Cars.* Full Throttle. Minneapolis: Bellwether Media, Inc., 2019.

Lanier, Wendy Hinote. *Indy Cars.* Let's Roll. Lake Elmo, MN: Focus Readers, 2017.

Let's Draw Vehicles with Crayola! Crayola! Minneapolis: Lerner Publications, 2018.

Indianapolis Motor Speedway Kids Club Website
www.indy500kids.com

Infographic: The Speed of Race Cars
www.childrensmuseum.org/blog/infographic-speed-race-cars

Zippy Facts about the Super Fast Honda Indy Car Race
www.cbc.ca/kidscbc2/the-feed/honda-indy-fun-facts

GLOSSARY

complete (kuhm-PLEET)— to finish

dangerous (DEYN-jer-uhs)—involving possible harm or death

engine (EN-jin)—a machine that changes energy into mechanical motion

lap (LAP)—one time around or over a course

turbocharged (TUR-bo-charjd)—having a device that increases an engine's power

INDEX

F

features, 4, 7, 8–9, 20, 21

H

history, 19, 21

S

safety, 13, 19
speeds, 6–7, 16, 19

T

tracks, 4, 10, 11, 14–15, 20